T0113828

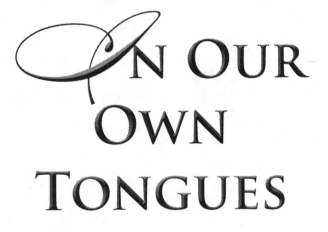

IN OUR

OWN

TONGUES

IN OUR OWN TONGUES

by *Fabu*
Madison Poet Laureate

University of Nairobi Press

First Published 2011 by University of Nairobi Press
3rd Flr. Jomo Kenyatta Memorial Library Bldg
University of Nairobi
P.O. Box 30197 – 00100 Nairobi, Kenya
E-mail: nup@uonbi.ac.ke   **Web: www.uonbi.ac.ke/press**

The University of Nairobi Press supports and promotes University of Nairobi's objectives of
discovery, dissemination and preservation of knowledge, and stimulation of intellectual and cultural
life by publishing works of highest quality in association with partners in different parts of the world.
In doing so, it adheres to the University's tradition of excellence, innovation and scholarship.

The moral rights of the authors have been asserted.

© *2011 Fabu Carter Mogaka*

All rights reserved. Except for the quotation of fully acknowledged short passages for the purposes of
criticism, review, research or teaching, no part of this publication may be reproduced, stored in any
retrieval system, or transmitted in any form or means without a prior written permission from the
University of Nairobi Press.

University of Nairobi Library CIP Data
In our own tongues / by Fabu B.C.
1. African American — Poetry. 2. American Poetry — Women
authors. 3. African American Women — Poetry
PS 591.N4I3

ISBN 9966 846 75 1 — 978 9966 846 75 4

Front Cover Photo Credit and Copyright: Franklynn Peterson

Cover layout, typography and book design by:
Calluna Graphic Design, LLC
203 1/2 E. Main St., Mt. Horeb, WI 53572, USA
(608) 437-2424.   www.callunagraphics.com

Printed by Sitima Printers and Stationers, P.O. Box 53987, Nairobi - 00200, Kenya

"For we are God's poems..."
Ephesians 2:10

Dedicated to
Woodie Onkendi
who inspires me to be more and write more
just because of the wonderful son that you have been
from your birth

and to

our fourth generation child/woman
Mauricia Lynn
may you be even more than the women in our family
could dream or live.

ᴛABLE OF CONTENTS

I Speak Swahili, Standard and Southern English 59

ᴀɴTRODUCTION

My journey to write, In Our Own Tongues began when I traveled to Nairobi, Kenya
from the University of Wisconsin-Madison to conduct research for my PhD
dissertation, which compared the African American Dozens and Toasts to Kissii
Joking Relationships. When I attached myself to the Department of Literature
at The University of Nairobi as a visiting scholar, it was shortly after Ngugi wa
Thiong'o had been forced out of the department by the Kenyan government.
Ngugi insisted on writing literature and staging plays in Kikuyu, one of the original
languages of the Kenyan people. He believed that African literature should be
written in African languages. His decision to write in his mother's tongue first, and
the revolutionary implications to African literature caused me to think deeply about
the words that I had grown up listening to since I was a child in the South.

Scholars have explored African American retentions of African languages and language
patterns, especially the well-researched Gullah/Geechee people in South Carolina
and Georgia. I believe that despite all the horrors of African American enslavement,
culture and language were not obliterated but rather transformed through the slave
experience. Ngugi's discourse on language awoke in me memories of how different
generations of Southern Black women spoke, as well as how I communicate with
people in this world. In Our Own Tongues gives poetic voice to three generations of
African American women and a variety of their experiences in the United States.
These were experiences with emotional, physical and sexual assaults, racism, lynching,
politics, as well as the permeating smell of magnolias. This collection explores both
the sadness and joy that were experienced living in Panola County, Holly Springs and
Como, Mississippi; Ft. Benning, Georgia, Memphis, Tennessee; Little Rock, Arkansas,
Nairobi, Kenya and Madison, Wisconsin.

In Our Own Tongues celebrates how Black women speak and do in the ways best known to us. My maternal grandmother was Effie Florida Cunningham Partee. She was born in Holly Springs, Mississippi and died in Como, Mississippi. My Grandmother Spoke African with a Bit of Southern English begins with her early 1900's generation, how she spoke, what she spoke about and the historical context of her life. The poems in the first section chronicle my Grandmother Effie and her age mates. My mother was Bernice Partee Carter, called "Hattie Mae" until she married my soldier father. She was born in Como, Mississippi, lived in many countries in the world and died in Madison, Wisconsin. My Mother Spoke Southern English with a Bit of African looks at the next generation, born in the mid 1900's and their strides for victory over racism and segregation that affected their language choice. These poems include poems of language assimilation. I Speak Swahili, Standard and Southern English, as a woman born in the late 1900's, completes the circle back to Africa and African language. I learned to be multilingual, multicultural and to fit, as my Black woman self, in this country and in this world. I learned this from Grandmother Effie and my Mama Bernice who were my first and most loving teachers.

Ngugi wa Thiong'o is rich in understanding that the language you first love and learn to speak in, is the most creative. I had the pleasure of hearing a mixture of African words and syntax in my grandmother's conversations to me. I truly loved hearing the joyful southern lilt in my mother's voice when she spoke with pride about her children and grandchildren. I now hear my own voice in the world, as well as speaking my grandmother's and my mother's tongues. Amen.

—Fabu Carter Mogaka

My Granny

Effie Florida Cunningham Partee

My Granny Spoke African with a Bit of Southern English

Like seedy cotton inside a beige hull
Grandma Effie was a sturdy southern plant
thrivin despite hot sun and burnin segregation
watered from an ancient well and female sweat
my Granny spoke African with a bit of southern English.

Chiren best 'member dat family be more den youren lives

Grandchildren heard her curious words
felt her devotion but didn't always understand her meanin.
My Granny survived livin colored in Como, Mississippi
to teach us how to speak her tongue
talkin' African in America.

IS 'MERICA

One day
we be in village
livin n free
livin n free.

Nex thin
come buckra slavers
carryin death
in long shiny chains.

Souls begin dyin
from first chains
pon we necks arms feets
we cry out for help
in many many tongues.

Buckra* starves n beats we
walks we walks
til feets be bleedin
walks we walks
to where we not know.

On ship
we rot n stink below
mens wimens chirens
mamas wid belly full of chile
all hate every rockin
dat take us far from home.

Sellin block
we no remember
small pain
agin de trip cross de ocean
we people piled high
in water graves.

Massa starves n beats we
works we works
til hands be bleedin
works we works
for why we not know.

Already hearts is dyin
from first chained feets
step pon dis land
dis 'Merica.

*Buckra is an African word
meaning white people.

16

Be a Woman/ She Be a Woman

Part I

i be so skeered breaths jerkin my body
when massa start payen me special attenshion
i doesnt knows whut to do
but i tries to act dumb n not understandin
all de same
i gets away from round him soonest possible
i skats down a different cotton row n pick dere
come sundown i heads for de quarters
i rubs my hands ober n ober ober n ober
i moans i groans i rolls round on de dirt floor
i gets up n goes out back de slave quarters
i throws soil pon my face n pon my head
i falls down wid my eyes turnt
towards ouren home cross de waters
i snatches n tears my hairs by dey roots
    Lawd why me whymewhymeme
not a white mans interest in me.

17

PART II

i all alone i gots no family left
ma n pa is dead wid de rest sold
long time we chiren was sold apart
eben so deres no law n no one to protect we
whut white craves white gits
it is we to suffer

   but why me why

ise a field woman i be coal BLACK
my hairs short short
buckra aint suppose to like we kind

   so why me me
i smells sweat cause i slaves
sunup/sundown in de cotton fields
i cant hab no buckra chirens milk white minders
to show my shame
i don't want no buckra chirens to uglify my name.

Part III

three four day pasted
den massa go n touch me
whilst i bends low pickin cotton
he feel my behind

i rears up n runsrunsrunsrunsrunsrunsrunsrunsruns
rite away de oberseer take after me hollarin
   GIT BACK HEAH NIGGA GAL
   GIT BACK TO WORK

i runs de faster ise screamin n runnin
runnin thru de cotton field trampin cotton rite n left
other slaves looks away n gits back outta my way
dey knows n i knows
whether i runs forward or back
i runnin to trouble i runnin to trouble.

i runs anyhow only faster n faster fasterfasterfaster
i runs for de big house
i runs toward missy ann
i runs wid out knowin i runs justa screamin n cryin
n half way thinkin

i be a woman n she be a woman

i be a woman n she be a woman.

PART IV

i throws myself down at missy ann feets
i pantin heavin cryin
    cryincryincryincryincryincryin
i begs i begs i begs her i begs her
    mam miss mam please sabe me
    sabe me from shame please miss mam
    please missy ann sabe me from de shame
    massa want me
    massa aim to take me
    massa gonna bed me aginst my will
i breaks into big sobs of please mam ober n ober n ober
    pleasemampleasemampleasemam
i clutches her skirts i bows lowly den looks up yet pleadin
n missy ann commence to spit in my face
she hak up all de spittle she can
n she spit
    she spit n spit she spitspitspit
in my face so long so much so mean her spittle cober my tears.

PART V

de others reaches de big house
i dragged outside striped naked n hanged by my wrists
missy ann whip my nakedness furst

    NIGGER
    HOW DARE YOU SAY MY HUSBAND WANTS YOU
    NIGGER GAL
    I'LL TEACH YOU TO TELL SUCH LIES
    MY HUSBAND WOULD NEVER TOUCH
    A BLACK NIGGER SOW

all de time de whip lash me eber where eber spot eber where
in her hands de whip lash

    lash lash lash lash lash lash lash lash

i far gone i don scream no more
i don beg i don moan i don groan
i thinks now massa will neber hab nothin
no more to want from me
i don eben feels de lash no more

i just hears de cush cush cush of de whip in my torn flesh

    cushcushcushcushcushcush
    cushcushcushcushcushcush

den dere is buzzin in my head n i kinda pass out
i don eben feels
when i lowered bleedin n bloody to de ground
n rite dere massa take my virginity.

21

TRILOGY OF RAPE

PART I
SLAVERY
"THE RAPE OF LITTLE SISTER"

Round baby fat rump
slightly tiltin towards de sky
Little sister
was out back
kinda squat down
tee teein.

Long came Massa roundin de corner
shoulda turn back
cause sista's butt was still in de air.
Stead he wait patiently
til she finish shakin herself dry
then he drap his pants
n ease up on her.

Lay down little sis
lay down n let me in
dont matta dat youre ten
don't matta dat youre kin.

PART II
RECONSTRUCTION
"THE RAPE OF LITTLE SISTER'S DAUGHTER"

Mr. Mott came by last nite
tole Big Buck he had three day work for 'im
three day work turnin over de land
at de ole Lee plantation.

Mr. Mott came by de nex nite
throwed Big Buck's wife down
on her Mama's red quilt pallet
'bused EmmaJean for hours
rite dere in front of her screamin babies.

Mr. Mott came by anuther nite
Buck came back early too
ole Mr. Mott is dead
dey lynch Buck
put his manhood in a mason jar
ta save de South.

PART III
POST RECONSTRUCTION
"THE RAPE OF LITTLE
SISTER'S GRANDDAUGHTER"

Sadie struggle de black way
hard n long
ta go ta school.
Education will take ya far
in dis heah world her ma say.

Furst one in de family
ta git much learnin.
Sadie teach colored
at de Normal school.
Lawd how she make us'es proud her grandma say.

Ah Sadie with her clever mind
n amber eyes
We live to see ouren womenfolk risen
from de slave fields to de schoolhouses.

De principal, uh Boston carpetbagger
keeped her late one evening.
He had his way wid da po chile
on de schoolroom floor.

Raped grandma.
Raped ma.
Raped grandchile.
Sadie say They relieve themselves in us.
We just like the outhouse
to be shit in.

The Mary Turner Lynching in Valdosta, Georgia

based on an eye witness report by Walter White,
N.A.C.C.P. Executive Secretary, 1918

Mrs. Mary:
colored mens privates
pickled n floatin in rubbin alcohol in a mason jar
sittin rite dere out front de counter
nex ta de candy balls for all de folks ta see
cause old man Sheehan
what runs de Valdosta General Store
say dat keep niggas in line
lynchin is dey way of life
lynched is ouren way of death

still n all me be hopin
dat hate fill crackers die out
n lil less hate eber generation
me be thinkin too
dat ifen me be real quiet real humble
all de time special round whites
dey wont pay me n mine no notice
dese whites wont visit dey calamity
pon me n mine
me work hard eber day ta be a mouse

nothin here ta speak of fur us'es
in valdosta georgia
ceptin hard work n us'es do dat eberday
ceptin de Lords day
me neber spect nothin fine from life
but live work eat n get a lil extra sleep
befo Sunday mornin service
n ta stay outta de way of lynchin whites
me reckon God see fit ta bless me special
fur de old ones sake
me jump de broom rite after harvest season 1918
wid a gooder man me neber know

togedder usen sharecrop 1 ½ acre
of mostly po rocky soil
my man lows how he can make do
n produce crops outta fields what most stone
him work de fields n me work de house

us'es works hard hard but dat taint nothin new
n now us'es be workin fur a furst born
me be feelin de stir of life widin me
us'es feel alrite causa us'es got each n oder

it were a clear satdiddy when my man
went off into town fur provision buyin
him kiss me twice on each cheek
n promise fur ta brin me molasses balls
on causa me cravin sweetin
him laff on down de road n swear
a sweet molasses gal chile is on de way from heben
causa ya eatin sweetin sweetin sweetin
me laff too it be good ta laff togedder
n me lows how him bedder come home quick quick to me

me were sittin on de front porch
shellin crowder peas fresh from de garden
wid de dew still a'clingin
me were hummin n thinkin life aint dat bad ebertime
ifen ya hav someone ta share wid
me see outta me thoughts dust risin justa balla dust risin
me says ta me wonder who dat be runnin lika dat
causa plenty folk liv up n down dis dirt road
it be marta boy n he lika falls at my feets

miz turner miz turner mam
dey say come ma say ya come
strate away to ouren house
come miz turner come

n den de boy grabin n jerkin my arms
well rite dere me almos ta die
me start wonderin who trouble fall on dis time
n whut de trouble is
me don't wait fur nothin me hurry so fast wid martha boy
askin
boy whut wrong boy
whut wrong
it be ma or pa sis or bro

martha n wimens is waitin only wimens
millin round in circles in de house when me gits dere
me know rite den dis trouble is lynchin calamity

me take off runnin fur de town
me don't know how me run fast or git dere so quick quick
whut wid belly full of chile

me see my man hangin lynched dead he dead
me see my man my husband a gooder man me neber did know
crackers don kilt my man
dose crazy crackers don brought dey calamity ta my door n knock
my man is lynched he eyes hang out he be purple blue dark n red
RED RED RED RED RED RED RED
blood eberwhere

he be just like Jesus
in de middle of two oders
me cuss n wail wail n cuss n waillllllllllllllllllllllllllllllllllllllll
me cuss dis white race fur generations ta come
me wail fur my gone man my gone life my gone luv
n my unborn baby chile wid no papa ta know
me scream
fur de soul of a good man lynched
battered n purpled swingin in de open
me screamin n stretched strate out
rite dere in front of dem white killers

n me know when dey begins murmurs
me hear dem say kill her too
let her join de bastid she cry for
n me feel ouren peoples try ta pull me away from dey evil
many colored peoples try n drag me from out in front de tree
afore dese crazy crackers kill me too

me know eberthin but me no move
me is rooted neath my man rooted widin a ancient wail
let me die wid him
let us'es three die family
causa whut sense it be ta liv mongst crazy crackers like dese?

southern gentlemens hangs me by my feets
dey lovely wimens cut my belly open n dey nicey chirens laff
de law sheriff step up n crush my baby head under his left boot
ole Sheehan happily throwin gasoline on my clothes
dey begins ta argue who will throw de first match
n me feel fire rise up n melt me

n ifen me aint dead enuf
dese whites riddle whut left of me wid bullets
my man up on nuther branch lynched
me charred n blacken wid bullet holes n dryin blood
belly split wide open
n my baby girlchile broken at my feets
wid her birthin cord tite betwixt us
de Turner family
from Valdosta Georgia[*]
me made de decision not ta be a mouse.

[*]Over 500 Black people left Valdosta,
Georgia after Mary and her baby girl
were lynched.

EFFIE IN THE COTTON FIELDS

Mississippi sky is stretched out blue
in the glimpse before headin out
most times barefooted
trampin on chilled, dewy ground
finally arrivin
at rows of ghostly fields.

No one sees dark turn light
except your hands become clearer
as they work the earth
the cotton bolls stick and cut your fingers
pullin softness out from prickly hulls.

You can't get no red on the fluff
so you suck your hurt fingers
while the other hand continues pickin row after row
the boys pickin cotton
while baby sister chops weeds.

Effie Florida Cunningham is in the fields
blackish curls tied up in a flour sack square
sunburned limbs bent over pullin weeds
thick round growin cotton stalks
tall from seeds that elder brother planted in Spring.

As she sweats and her back hurts
Effie is the fields dreamin
one day sharecroppers own land
one day pickers get more money
from the real price of cotton.

One day colored folks sell at the Exchange
and one day Pa might just buy me a pretty
something fine on store credit
iffin this year we don't owe more than we made
iffin this year.

Rufus Cunningham & Ida Curry's Baby Girl

Spirit turned flesh
in another virgin's womb
from a Methodist preacher father

Iridescent eyes reflected sun, land and rain
pale skin with flecks of yella
short and slight.

Curly hair deeply black
slicked down with Royal Crown*
hated it long.

Private thoughts left unsaid
soft voice
that fussed a lot.

Goodman, Robert, Fred and Leroy
Effie's brothers
big sisters Thelma, Mary and a never known baby.

All could pass for white
all decided to stay Black
just because they were.

Twenty-one years
then she married
never wanted no man but Woodie Partee.

*Royal Crown is a brand of hair "grease" in the South.

Woodie Partee's Promise

He didn't want no rascal like me botherin his daughter
On account of him bein a preacher man

Effie and me were courtin strong
But we had to meet a ways from her home

I courted her anyway sittin on Mr. Jeb's fence
I'd prop her on top and stand facin her

Lookin into clear eyes that did not stop
Effie heard my heart and strong desire

My promise was not to be a faithful husband
The best provider or a wonderful father but

If Effie was sittin on a fence and fell
I'd catch her before she hit the ground.

Sunday 1949
in Como, Mississippi

White grits circlin in boilin water, softenin
over a hot smoky flame
she adds salt and pepper pinches
measured in the palm of her hand
then scoots outside in the early dark
to the smoke house for the last slab of bacon.

Smallish feet on a grass worn path
her grey eyes adjust to the deep blackness
returnin the same twenty-seven steps to her kitchen
she picks up the large wooden spoon
stirrin thickenin grits into smooth
she slides the cast iron pot back to a lower flame
and lifts up the heaviest skillet
to fry thick pieces of pork
thinkin briefly how this last hog fed the family well.

More things left like gatherin eggs
pourin sorghum over last night's biscuits
addin fresh churned butter to done grits
before the smells alert eight bodies
to Sunday mornin breakfast
more things left like layin out good clothes
washin up and dressin seven little bodies
fussin with Woodie before she can finally get dress
for service at Mt. Moriah church.

A rooster screams at the risin sun
Effie pauses her thoughts
then walks to the open back door
she breathes in heavy country silence
sings a little of Give Me Jesus*

In the mornin when I rise
In the mornin when I rise
Give me Jesus
Give me Jesus
You may have the world
Give me Jesus.

She sings, then hums before Sunday busyness and family begins.

*Give Me Jesus is an African American folk song called a
spiritual that all the Cunningham children learned from their
father, Reverend Rufus Cunningham.

Of He Suit Me, He Outta Suit You

Effie ate coal
instead of drinkin cream
in her marriage
which ran hot and cold
but seldom warm
or enough.

Woodie knew
two outside women
one birthed his son
before his marriage
another birthed his daughters
when his marriage was old.

Effie knew
her seven children
never did
til they were grown
heard the talk
and went lookin.

Woodie used words
to build a fence
around his pride
but his boys and girls
hated what he done
to his face.

Effie gathered them
to hear her voice
definite
bout her husband's cheatin
Iffen he suit me
he outta suit you.

Their Children's
Response

Their Children's Response

Woodrow:	Like well cooked okra
Fred:	boiled with a bit of salt
Ethel:	your words
Bernice:	slide down our throats
James:	sticky
Mattie:	sensation
Robert Earl:	all the way.

Magnolia Smile

What Miss Effie taught
growin up
ceptin to always smile
that magnolia smile
waxy white
with a little yella inside.

My Mama

Bernice Partee Carter

My Mama Spoke Southern English with a Bit of African

Churned pale yellow butter from fresh cow's milk
is how Mama spoke.
Her young skin scorching in fields picking cotton
out of four bales, three for Mr. Taylor
one for family.
Mama kept memories she never told.
Teen bride of an army soldier from the North
she ran hard into marriage
escaping seasonal schooling and Jim Crow laws.

Mrs. Rosa Parks' Decision on December 1, 1955

Early morning at home:
i was talking to Jesus
long
about how we suffering so
in the South.

High noon at work:
i remembered strength
in my mother
in my grandparents'
lives.

Late evening at the bus stop:
i'm tired of getting on the bus
a scary voice
making me move
always back.

Made up mind:

i reckon to put to use
what i learned at Highlander*
act nonviolent
but insist on what is right.

Sitting down for freedom:

i knew I was strong too
No white man! Not today
nor tomorrow
either.

In an Alabama jail:

i was not alone
more names than can be said
jailed for our freedom
we were determined.

*The Highlander Folk School is a leadership training and cultural center located in Tennessee. Mrs. Rosa Parks was trained there prior to her historic role in the Civil Rights movement.

41

The Daughter Who Became Real After Her Daddy Died

Ahh, the duplicity of little white lies.
Strom Thurmond, active segregationist
and defender of the racist South, enjoyed a little white lie
from the time he was a young lawyer ravishing the teenage nigra help
not once but many times, as she worked in his Mama's kitchen
until, in lily-white estimation, the worst of all worst was birthed
a child, who was certainly not white or real to them
living proof that mis-ce-ge-nation does exist.

Ahh, the duplicity of little white lies.
A girlchild looking like Strom birthed her himself
with his broad forehead, beak nose and well
American reporters asked Essie Mae for almost 70 years,
"Is Strom Thurmond your Daddy?" but never once asked the
honorable Senator
"Do you have a daughter with a Black woman?"
cause little white lies are like puffs of cigar smoke
now you see them but pretend you don't
while the bitter smell remains.

Ahh, the duplicity of little white lies.
How does a daughter answer the obvious little white lie
with Mama dead
and furtive visits through the back doors
for check-ins with such a great white man
and his occasional envelopes of money
for schooling, keeping quiet and such
cause rape is not rape when nigra females

from children to elders work in white homes.
Rape is listed in the interview with Mrs. Southern Ladies
under "other duties as required."

Ahh, the duplicity of little white lies.
Better forget that pain and shame that runs wet down generations
of Southern Black women
otherwise Essie Mae Thurmond Washington
it is your fault that you were ever born.
To acknowledge this daughter's birth threatens southern traditions
and the greatness of the rebel South.
As the good ole boys from South Carolina would say
"Ya'll know Strom busted hell wide open."

MARCHING WITH REV. DR. MARTIN LUTHER KING JR.

Strong in her wants from birth, Mattie called Sister is the baby girl with parents and six others telling her who to be and what to do. When she became African in her dress, hair, and thoughts, well we listened to make sure good sense was talking outta her young mouth. Sister made like she was marching with Reverend King and nobody better try stop her.

People forget that Reverend King's voice was fed by millions of whispers. Black folks whispering across America. In the cotton fields of southern towns. In the factories of northern cities. In prisons or in public. In shotgun houses, tenement buildings and projects, folks whispered This ain't right how we treated.

Reverend King's voice gave sound to the tongues of our grandfathers and grandmothers silenced by lynching, segregation and the terror of Klu Klux Klan ghost riders. His voice gave sound to our fathers and mothers swallowing down racism and injustice again and again. This was the time when most were shut up or shut down by fear.

Mattie said she was marching and as the middle sister, I was marching too. The march began like the Mississippi river in flood season, folks spilling out everywhere. Reverend King was far up front with the "hoity-toities" and it was us, the hard working regulars, in the middle and the back.

His voice came in waves. Freedom ran through our veins causing us to march straighter and sing stronger. Then we heard shattering glass. Screams burst as tear gas popped, spreading quickly when Memphis police waded into the crowd swinging wooden batons, whacking brains and flesh.

The running began and we were pushed towards the river. I thoughtwesurelyjoiningtheancestorsatthebottom.Sistergrabbedmy hand and said we gonna make it. Blood in the streets. Folks limping and holding broken body parts. Paddy wagons stuffed with Black people. We are no longer deaf or mute but loud in remembering these times.

GEORGIA IN MY MIND

Darkly handsome Carter, my Army corporal husband, was stationed at Ft. Benning, Georgia. We were a young Negro family with no car, living in the city. One bus went back and forth. When he was restricted to the base, me and our babies visited on Saturdays to love and laugh together.

Say Georgia and some think of English prisoners released to fill up this state. Others think fat juicy peaches, fuzzy pink like the white folks, only the fruit is what is sweet. In my mind Georgia means bitter prejudice.

I recall the bus ride to the base, me with an arm baby and a knee baby. I carried Tony while Fabu was a toddler on skinny legs. The same bus driver was patient until I dropped coins in, clink, clink. Right after the last clink, that ugly man pressed the accelerator down hard.

The bus jerked fast making me and my babies almost fall. Georgia reminds me of the long trip to the back of the bus—rocking, lurching and clutching babies. The dead eyes of the white passengers and never their hands to help, as we wobbled our way to the colored section.

My daughter whining as she slipped in the fast moving bus. Anger heating my face as I used one hand for her and the other for my baby boy while a white bus driver tries his best to knock us to the floor; the wife and small children of an American soldier defending the rights of white folks like these to be free.

CLAY, DUST & DIRT

I've eaten clay and dirt.*
Best dirt is right up the road
on the hill by Miss Clara's house.

Yella dirt is sour
While orange clay is sweet.
I mix em together
for the best lip-full in Panola County.

And well, you can't help
but eat dust in Mississippi.
It cover the land, trees
and the water. If I stood real still
dust would cover me.

That's all right though,
cause ain't nothing ever died
from just clay, dust and dirt.

*Southern African American women often "eat" dirt and clay when
pregnant. This spread from Africa to the U.S. In Africa the most commonly
ingested nutrients in dirt and clay were phosphorus, potassium, magnesium,
copper, zinc, manganese and iron.

$\mathcal{S}$OUTHERN LOVE

I want love to be like a good pot of greens
pick the tenderest parts
separate from the hard stem
wash gently and thoroughly
removing every bit of dirt and grime
rinsing over and over and over
with the clear clean water of forgiveness
season with savory meat, herbs and spices
and then simmer, simmer, simmer.

UMMIN IN THE SHADE

Mississippi man puta hummin in you
way down your belly.

A hummin
make grape kool-aid taste like hot sauce
and your collard greens smell like peach cobbler.

A hummin
make the mind dis-recollect
that sunrise bring too much hard work
and shit to shineola* for pay.

A hummin
make you break your plate*
get up from the table full
cause he lived to come home whole.

Mississippi man puta hummin in you
reminder that dark is good.

*"Shit to Shineola" and "Break Your Plate" are both
African American sayings. The first refers to shineola, a
type of black shoe paste. When you "break your plate"
means whenyou are finished and can't go back to it.

WALKING WITH BIG MAN

Big Man stops us walking by the curve in the road
and I ask, You got a stone in your shoe?
He just reaches over into a dusty bush
grabs warm, plump, muscadines*
brushing them carefully with his pocket rag.

Big Man leans fingers against my lips, open in surprise
squeezes hot juice into my mouth
purple sliding to my chin
and the tartness makes me mmmmmmm with pleasure.

Big Man wipes my skin with the fabric's clean side
and I smell ivory soap in both nostrils.
As we laugh together and start back walking
I say, Big Man you so good to me.

*Muscadines are a purple grape variety with a thick
skin and musky smell.

UDDEN BEAUTY
FOR VICKI

Southern girls like planted crops
grow succulent
with sun and well water.

Southern soil bursts open
like young girls straining
to become women quickly.

Southern girls like harvested crops
ravished
for the tastes of men.

IGHTENING
GIRL

Struck with power
standing wet under a solitary tree
in a wide green pasture.

Even electric bolts
didn't scare her, slow her down none
just bothered her some.

Flashing out of her mouth
for the rest of her life
were words that shocked and stunned.

BERNICE AT FOURTEEN

Against a dated backdrop of flowered curtains
A girl woman stands
With sparkling skin the color of white gold.

In the straight back and hand on one hip
Is pride and defiance from a middle daughter
Who very early made herself known
As special and strong and utterly sassy.

Dark eyes face a future
Innocently unaware that fourteen will be
Her absolute last year of childhood.

The next year her youthful shapely body
Swelled with child the same way her finger tightened
Inside a gold plated wedding band
From a Northern soldier boy.

Bernice at fourteen
Stands in a yellowing photograph
More beautiful than my words can ever say.

SOUTHERN
GRITS WOMAN

Right size cast iron pot
boiling water
grits measured
by heart and hand
stirring quickly
with a wooden spoon
add a pinch of salt
from an African sea
and just churned butter
from fresh sweet milk.

Chicken Frying Life Lessons

Mama
though a 1950's bride
never liked cooking no how
but still taught her two girls
how family fries chicken.

She said,
chicken lets you know
when to turn it over
if you rightly hear that certain hum
not just chicken frying sounds.

We Black folks
listen for what others
don't hear and don't hafta hear.
They chicken burn, they get another
or go out to eat.

Our chicken
got to last, stretch and taste good for us.
Do the same with white folks
listen for that certain hum
not words they never say out loud.

ER DYING SON

With the same tenderness
she held him at birth
his mother held him
as he died.

In a surprise moment
he was born
In the middle of life
he passed on.

Suffering turned him
away from pride.
He lived fuller at the end
than his beginning.

EET ME IN HEAVEN

was handwritten
on lined paper
in her beautiful looping style
simple and direct
defying western popular culture
ignoring atheist cacophony
obliterating denominational predilections.

For Our Travelin Sister Hattie

And the travelers walked through the byways… Judges 5:6

Sister Hattie has on her travelin shoes.
She done left the main road of this here life
and is walkin through the byways.

Sister Hattie has on her travelin shoes
and is gone to a far better place
where joy is constant and pain no more.

Arise, arise and sing a new song of love
for our travelin Sister Hattie
who is now walkin through the byways.

ERNICE SMELLS MAGNOLIAS

Ride in the tree swing
     over and done

She stands up pleased
      flexing dusty toes

Penetrating noon sun
     on emerald kudzu*

Circles of sweat dampen
     her thin dress

She hears a truck bumping
     down the rock road

One brown plait undone
     her shoes inside

She runs to the door
     then looks back
Lingering to quickly inhale
     the scent of magnolias.

*Kudzu is a green vegetation from Japan that invaded
and covered the trees in the South.

57

Myself

Fabu Carter Mogaka

I Speak Swahili, Standard & Southern English

Grandma Effie and her African ways cultivated me
as I trailed her round her rake pattern yard
pushing flowers into cut-off bleach bottles and every size jelly jars
dropping seeds into tilled Mississippi black dirt
watching her open beauty in the earth.

My Mama's southern lilt, taught me early to speak words
because she was a woman determined never to be silenced.
Yet, even Mama was uneasy when I spoke loud
bout hush hush family secrets
I grew knowing words are power in an honest women's mouth.

I speak Swahili, standard and southern English
mimininaongeakiswahili,kiingerezachakawaidanakiingerezachakusini,Ya'll
I also speak in tongues.
Poet synthesis of African heat and magnolia perfume, I am
recreated from the tongues of both mothers.

WOMEN WARRIORS

ONE. THE PEASANT.
FOR WANJIKU WA MUKABI AND
SARAH WAMBUI MUKABI

We were working the plot. The grass was high
after three days of rain.
Our backs were bent low in gratitude. There would
be crops to harvest, food to eat.
They came silently. We did not hear them
because of the mud and their soft shoes.
They grabbed him roughly an old man their father.
I screamed loudly beating one with my hoe.
He slapped me hard, threw me into the mud.
Old man, I cried, Are we to meet an undignified death today?
I spoke to the wind. Those young thugs had taken him
to a car, shoved him in. He could say nothing.
Not even good-bye. He could do nothing but mumble
against their hands.

Our sons ran with weapons
to fight the intruders.
Aiiieee, the strangers have taken out guns.
What is this that has visited our poor homestead?
City men with cars and suits and guns.
One is yelling to our sons
We are Special Branch, Kenyan Secret Police!
We are taking this one into custody! Do not come closer!

Our daughters help me rise from the mud.
I look into their frightened faces. What is cus-to-dy?
The local chief has arrived.
The old father stares bewildered from behind the glass window.
Old man, the chief hisses. Old man, traitor, didn't I tell you
not to talk against the Government? Now you will feel
the strength of its hand.
Our daughters scream.
Our sons moan, drop their weapons and look at their toes.

We are old people, I cry up to the sun.
Who calls him a traitor in a free country?
With patriotic words, whom has he betrayed?
With patriotic words, what thing has he hurt?
This father fought in the forests. He was detained
by the colonialists. Me and my children starved for Uhuru
this country's freedom. What madness is this talk of traitor?

Careful old woman, Special Branch warns, or we will take you.
Our prisons are too full, overflowing with things like you!
The car speeds away. I send my spirit to comfort my husband.
I stumble to our home.
I get the small money, fold it, place it between my breasts.
I will follow the old man, wherever he is taken.

At the shops, the villagers stare as if I am crazed.
Someone advises, Better to leave him old Mama.
If he has done nothing, he will not be punished.
If? If, for a man born in this village. His clan is known

for their farming skills and the honesty in their hearts.
Others come forward to say the strangers came to them
asking about the old man. What he said. What he did.
They told them harmless stories.
But why, I ask, Didn't you tell us?
There is silence for an answer.

The sky becomes noisy.
As it rains I search for a vehicle to hire
to take me to my old man.
Together we will survive this too.

TWO. THE CIVIL SERVANT.
FOR THE MWATELA FAMILY

I sleep in a cold bed. I walk through
an empty flat. I pretend that life is normal
as I care for our children. The father of my children
is gone. He is somewhere in the city hiding
trying to escape political henchmen.
I don't know where your father is
I mean, he had to go away for a while,
a business trip, yes, a business trip.
Eat your sukuma wiki children.

My heart is with you wherever you are
jumping at shadows, sleeping here, moving there
as you dodge
the men sent to whisk you into detention.
Father of my children, you are truly harassed
escaping the net they are surely encircling you with.

What have you done that your own
would hunt you like a Maasai stalks his first lion?
Are you a test for impotent manhood? Does a kinsman
eat his own? Who are these strangers in our midst?

We were proud when you became a civil servant.
Our family felt you would serve our nation well.
You served well, with honesty. Your reward
for commitment to a nation and to truth—PUNISHMENT!
You are forced to hide like a scurrying panya
instead of living upright like a man.

Nowadays who dares not to eat
from the table of greedy men? Even our President
eats full and well. You refused so they try to eat you
like roasted goat meat with their beer
to further stretch their bloated bellies.
These strange henchmen are watching
the bus stations, the train station, the airport.
They carry your recent photograph as they scour the city.
These strangers sit in your favorite bars
with your description burned into their eyes, waiting.

Hide well my husband. Hide deep into the earth
for not many will open their doors to you
because of their awful fear.
Don't let them find you. Please don't let them catch you.
Do not think of us your family. We can survive
on milk and maize meal.
When that is gone, I will send our children
to our parents in the rural areas, while I wait
in this silent flat for you.
I sleep in a cold bed. I walk through
an empty flat. I have nightmares of angry gods
sending vengeful demons to snatch our happiness.
It is midnight. I turn to my pillow, press my mouth
into the feathers to keep from screaming, Uhuru sasa.

THREE. THE INTELLECTUAL.
FOR MUMBI WA MAINA

There are strange men at my door
with hostile faces and evil intentions.
They wear business suits and pasted on smiles.
One calls my name and moves forward
too close to me. I cringe and draw back to ask
What is it you want? Who is in charge?

They want you, my friend and my husband.
My reason for leaving my parents' warmth.

I, also, part my lips and show my teeth.

He is not home. I don't know where Professor is.
Is it possible that my growing fear
has not been revealed? I must be strong.
I must be strong. I will not show my terror,
not to these puppet-men. I am not afraid of puppet-men
who follow orders without thinking or feeling.
I am afraid of the destruction of human lives
that puppet-men cause.

They have come for my darling, to drag him to a place
away from me and teaching and our life.
They want to search our home.
They want to poke among private items.
Other sounds escape their lips
but I have ceased to listen.
Oh how charming they try to appear
as they search everything and everywhere and every room
as they gather papers, books and even scraps.

Why am I here to face this insanity alone?
Where are our neighbors? Where are our colleagues?
Surely everyone sees what is happening at our home.
I see the crowd gathering to look as they take out boxes
again and again and again.
I insist that you write down each article
that you are taking and sign your names.
Whatdoyouhopetofindinthehomeoffacultybesidesnotes,
lessons, research and books?
Despair is creeping into my voice so I talk louder,

Why have you crept to our door? What have you slithered around this campus looking for? Why have you debased thisplaceoflearning?IfIclosemyeyes,wouldyoucurryback tothegovernmentgangstersandinsist,wecannotbeapart of such injustice?

They have finally left our home. I must quickly get word
to you my husband, not to return. But first, I'll sit here
for a few moments, just a few moments, to recapture the love
that this house has held for us. It seems that there
is never enough time to prepare for separation,
but I will swallow my tears. You must be protected
until we decide whether you go into exile or report
to the nearest police department.

My husband and I are intellectuals, teachers, writers,
I will not fool myself that those in power understand us.
But I trust that somebody will remember
that you whom this Government seeks to destroy
you are one of our country's true patriots.

Four. The Student.
For Katini Mwachofi and the memory
of Mwakdua Mwachofi

In the beginning, it was almost too much for my heart
to take. I had never seen people behind prison bars.
I had never seen people waiting to see people behind prison bars.
The experience was harsh and cruel and unforgettable.
Guards screaming curses. Women's faces full of anguish,
pleading to be allowed inside. Babies crying
because they too felt the horrible tension between the adults.
An old Mzee shoves close to the entrance gate to be among the few
in the crowd permitted to see loved ones. Most will not.
Guards are robot men wielding wooden batons. Robot men
forcing everyone to literally flee or be beaten.
It was in such a place that I first met you.

I was introduced to you through a dark screen,
only your profile was visible
only your voice seemed real.
You were struggling to talk normally to your youngest sister.

Your attempts to ease her fears, mixed with numerous
conversations, loud, in ethnic languages.
She pressed against the dark screen
as if her gesture would free you.
I stood back, trying not to hear, to give you both
a small sense of the privacy that the horrible conditions
refused to allow.

The jailers returned much too quickly. I know less than 10 minutes
passed. They forced everyone away from both sides of the mesh
screens. You and the other students moved down the passage
to return behind bars.

I turned to glimpse you thin and dirty, shoulders straight
against the sun. That moment froze in my memory.
I wondered about the contradiction
students in jail because they were students
studying the truth of what happened in their own country.

I came to visit you
because of your sister, my new friend.
I had recently arrived in the city, a first year student,
to attend University. I didn't know about up-country politics,
human rights or student versus government confrontations.
I was lonely and frightened to be away from my village
where we were wananchi who knew and cared for each other.
Your sister was kind to me. I returned her kindness
by accompanying her on weekly visits
to see her incarcerated brother.
I didn't realize that these visits would change my life.

I recall the day the students were released. Rather it was
a Presidential Pardon with the threat of future action. I ran,
forgetting my classes, past the campus celebrations and discussions
to your sister's home. I looked at a whole you and was confounded.
After almost a full year of remand, suffering was etched into
your face,

yet your eyes were still clear and your smile gentle.
I sat across from you and I listened intently as you spoke
of your torture at the hands of the prison guards.
I asked naive and foolish questions

Aren'tstudentssupposedtoquestionanddisagreewiththestatusquo?
Why should our government fear, harass and jail students
and citizens for their beliefs?

In the months to come, I learned answers to my own questions.
I met you on campus, in the company of other student
leaders. I wanted to stop you and say that I was no longer
an ignorant schoolgirl from the reserves. I understood the isms;
sexism, classism, racism, neo-colonialism, imperialism.
I intended to ask you how to get involved. I wanted to help.
I wanted to contribute to the country I loved too.
I never said anything. I continued to go to your sister's home sit
silently on the opposite couch, gazing at you, listening and learning.
I suppose it was then that I began to deeply respect your sacrifice.
Another student uprising. Many are hurt and raped, many have
died. This time the police beat me on my head, screaming

Youstupidstudents.Wemustbeatsenseintotheheadsyourefusetouse!

More students are picked up for interrogation and torture. They
have you again.

I fear that this time these men will kill you. It is suddenly not
enough to visit students in remand. It is not enough to moan and
cry about this terrible government.

I will take up where imprisoned student leaders have left off.
I am a woman.
I have been a quiet student. No one will suspect me of
hidden, rock-hard,
wanawake strength.

I have a regret. I never held your hand.
I never said I love you.
I never spoke of my respect and admiration
for you as one of our student leaders battling the system
throughout the years
of student-government fights.
Perhaps it might comfort you lying in a cold concrete prison cell
to know that your courage has inspired others,
and to know
you are not forgotten.
Perhaps, just perhaps, if I had spoken sooner or if you had
interpreted
my shy silence
we could have worked for our country's freedom, together.

Women Warriors was written in Kenya as I watched women from 1982 (the Kenyan Coup attempt) to 1986 fighting governmental oppression in their personal lives. These women, with the exception of Katina Mwachofi and Mumbi wa Maina, continue to live in Kenya and stand as warriors.

Swahili words:
Uhuru-freedom
Sukuma wiki – Kenyan national dish of kale.
Maasai-nomadic Kenyan ethnic group.
Panya-rat
Maize-corn
Uhuru sasa-freedom now
Mzee-elderly man
Wananchi-common folk
Remand-jail
Wanawake-women

I Am a Man:
Mr. Eugene Clemons

we come out of Mississippi
seekin more life, good schoolin
money to enjoy
leavin "nig" and sharecroppin behind.

at first a Memphis city job was real good
best was the benefits
what i care i'm a garbage man
been cleanin after white folks a long time.

trotted eight hours behind a truck
white man at the wheel
better than a mule's backside
and the chokin dust from dry fields.

city money didn't stop growin shame
bile in my throat bein called boy
I AM A Man in 1968
I wanna drive that garbage truck too.

we call on Dr. King for help
with the stalled sanitation strike
he answered, we marched
folks were beaten then he was murdered.

Lawd have mercy
the price was high
for poor, Black, mistreated trash men
to have the equal right to drive a garbage truck.

FROM A LITTLE
BROWN GIRL

Little brown ears heard up close
The Civil Rights movement
explained inside our home.

Mr. Clemons, fired sanitation worker
shared personal updates on the strike
connecting 1968 Memphis to 1955 Selma.

Daddy, career Army sergeant
ordered away from us to fight for freedom
for our country in Viet Nam.

Mommy, southern homemaker
gone into the streets to march for freedom
for our people in Memphis.

Little brown mind turning over and over
to understand
courageous parents and our country's rejection.

Daddy left first
to a place I could only reach
with my bedtime prayer, God please bless my Daddy.

Mommy said I could not march
along side of her
it was her time to fight, not yet mine.

Fear was heavy in me
lose Daddy in a faraway war
lose Mommy in a war up close.

Little brown eyes watched
on Easter morning
soldiers in tanks rumble through our neighborhood.

When the news came that Dr. King was murdered
Mommy's screams changed me forever
I stood as a little brown girl and whispered

Please Jesus, Let Mommy and Daddy live
Dr. King is dead
You could have taken me instead.

REVEREND DR. MARTIN LUTHER KING JR.

I saw you in a color photograph
with a fancy gold frame
on my Granny's living room wall.

You hung right beside Jesus
cause one was her King in heaven,
the other her King on earth.

She needed both, faith and action,
in sweltering Mississippi
to twist change into the rural South.

I read you in the books published by Ebony*
my Mama bought for us to read
about Reverend Dr. Martin Luther King Jr., Negro leader.

*Johnson Publications publish Ebony and Jet magazines and other
African-American books focused on the African American experience.

You were placed right beside the Holy Bible
cause when scripture was read and prayers said
she included you too.

She needed both prayer and knowledge,
living in a southern city
to demand the freedom that is her God given right.

Now that you are gone, our Reverend and our King
We still need your courage and your strength
living in this new millennium
where everything is considered right and nothing is wrong.

PRESIDENT BARACK OBAMA

He stands tall
against those times
when we were made to bend
again and again.

Strong
from thick roots
the black of his father
the white of his mother.

Confident
to convince a nation
and this world that he will lead
well.

Peace
reconciliation and hope
flow from his lips
and we believe him.

THIS WOMAN I LOVE

For Effie Florida Cunningham Partee

Down a winding dirt road
with rust colored rocks
and glistening beige pebbles
is where my grandmother lived.

She woke up to clear blue skies
and billowing white clouds.
My grandmother went to sleep
when the shimmering sun was just down
and the still stars were floating outward.

Yet all the beauty
of Mississippi land
cannot nearly compare
to this woman I love.

EARNING GRANNY STYLE

Crumpled wax paper
from tries at cutting perfect circles
to place at the bottom of two cake pans.

Crumpled wax paper
that looks like Grandma Effie's face
creased lines, light skin almost see-through.

Crumpled wax paper
trying to be great at baking
because my Grandma Effie teaches me how.

Finally smooth wax paper
round to the edges of both bottoms
making sure done cake doesn't stick.

Grandma says
Smooth wax paper
is like family
a lining of protection.
Saffron features

My Mother is
Bernice Partee Carter

Delicate and melting
High yella woman beauty.

Nuances in a lyrical voice
Calling my name
Over the years from childhood
To grown.

Sensation of textured skin
Our hands alike
Touching just to touch
And feel.

My hearts remembers yours
Beating
While I floated in your womb.

BREATHE
MY MOMMA

i breathe my Momma
sleepy face snuggling into her cotton dress
dried by hot sun and scented by cool wind
my head moves to a special Momma rhythm
my tiny body riding a swaying knee
fits across only one.

riding her knee like a slow song
moving from alert gurgling to cocooned silence
when her knee stops
heavy, heavy sleep uncurls my limbs
into flat and relaxed
i babysnore as my Momma lays me
in my lacy Sears & Roebuck Co. bassinet.

A Girl in My Mother's House

Sleep is sweeter than sugar cane, stripped and chewed,
in my Mother's house
where the electric fan whrrrrrrrs you to sleep
making my very bones drowsy
deeply sleeping on a pallet* thrown down on her bedroom floor.

The bed linen in my Mother's house
smells of southern spices, tangy red and black peppers,
clean comfortable resting
on Argo starched, crisp, ironed sheets
with chicken feather pillows that stick out and poke.

In my Mother's house are many feelings
some good like her fried sweet corn, others
bad tasting like the castor oil we swallow for worms
most unspoken and mixed, sweet and bitter like lemonade
even so there is love and peace and rest
best of all when I awake, my Mommy is there.

*A pallet is thick quilts or blankets laid on the floor for children
to nap and play on. Argo laundry starch is made from corn by
the Argo company. Southerners starch their clothes and eat it.

TEENAGER IN MEMPHIS

In my mother's home
are eighteen years of living
my particular splash of purple
against the beige, tan and cream
of her life.

She is the mother
and I am the child
no matter fifteen years of age difference
mellowing through the years
from bright to light.

Momma lets me be
an extraordinarily rare gift
that brings vividness
along with textured shades
to the interior of my life.

My Mother is Sun.
My Father Is Moon.

My mother is sun
Yellow heated passion
'ssippi hot
burning illumination.

My father is moon
Bright in still darkness
Glimmering cool
Contrary by day or moonless night.

And I am moving water
Reflecting sun and moon
Points of light
While my parents rest before rising.

LOOD KIN

As magnolia blossoms scented Holly Springs, Mississippi
we gathered
the blood kin of six alabaster brothers and sisters
cause the seventh one named Mary
never birthed.

I stood crowded with my kin
Seeing us repeated in each face
Knowing the red fire of their blood
Glowed crimson in me too.

i felt swishing inside like my first time in Africa
an immediate connection to people and land
our blood rushing hot
to quickly tell our stories.

then came cooling tears for the gone kin
as the sweet breath of our elders
reminded and rejoiced among us
our children danced and sang their newness
rooted in the Cunningham* past.

*Cunningham is my maternal grandmother Effie's maiden name and
our last family reunion was in 2008 after thirty-five years.

AMILY VISITS

it is through small rituals
that grandma and mama
visit me.

boiling grits
in the morning
picking and cleaning
greens for evening supper.

my hands
follow their work
my knees
bend to their faith.

the quilts
created
from their cotton dresses
cover me.

all that i do
reminds
that grandma and mama
come often to visit with me.

REAMLESS NIGHT

Before the sun's rays lightened the darkness
Cousin Cassandra stood by the window.

Curved and sad her back
Casting a bent profile
On the moon-drenched ceiling
Cassandra looking out at nothing
Sees too much.

Lowering the blinds
Snapping them shut
Turning to an empty bed
Cassandra thinks of her lover
Trudging a harsh white land.

Dedicatedtomytwocousinsnamed Cassandra:thefirstwhowasmy
friend,dormroommateandwhodiedmuchtooyoungandthesecondwho
has yet to fully live her life.

HOLDING TIME

I hold time, touching the happiness of the past
when we were alive together
Granddaddy Woodie, Grandma Effie, Uncle James,
Cousin Cassandra, my brother Tony, Mama and me
smiling in a 1970 photograph in Como, Mississippi.

This photo places me smack in the middle
of that summer day
our stomachs swollen with fresh garden watermelon
eating and being family together
with little thought except our contentment.

Mama and me are the only ones left to look
thirty-four years later at this black and white Polaroid
and she is threatening to leave too
she whispers confidences to Grandma Effie, deceased in 1976
when she thinks that I don't hear.

I hold time, tracing our smiles with my fingertips.

GLIMPSING UNCLE JAMES

Eyes slanted towards the sun
Kindness etched like tribal markings
On ochre skin burning black in summer
Sinewy with grace and skills
Secretive in wants and desires.

Married young to his choice of wife, not his sisters
She was a country woman with a boy child
Added three children before Ma and kids left for Chicago
Before an encounter between an oak tree and his raggedy car
Left him buried in Mississippi dirt.

I glimpsed you seven years later
At a bus stop near a Nairobi roundabout
Familiar shiny skin with curved eyes
I hollered Uncle James
The man paused, smiled
Then disappeared into the crowd.

ᏚONY MAURICE CARTER: A LITANY OF REMEMBRANCE

SUPPLICATION ONE: LET MY BROTHER LIVE IN ME

Do not let me forget
Him whom I cherish
Gone in body
He shall live
In memory and in heart.

SUPPLICATION TWO: THIS BITTER CUP

The prognosis is poor
And we hate her words
Who believes Doctors give life.

There is nothing that can be done
Is the second medical opinion
And three women weep.

Grieving mother, wife and sister
Refuse to drink
From this cup of bitter medicine.

SUPPLICATION THREE:
WE TRIED TO STOP DEATH

If death could be tricked
We'd have never let it take you
Take one of us instead.

If death could be wrestled
We'd have pinned it down
So it would never get up.

If death could be thwarted
We'd have whipped it bad
Till kingdom come.

SUPPLICATION FOUR:
PLEASE DON'T DIE YOUNG

Two tears ran down the sides of your face
Not so quickly that I didn't see
And mourning burst again in my belly.

As I stood amongst pinging machines
My hands reached out to stop the flow
Nurse is quick to say He doesn't feel pain
It is his tear ducts lubricating his eyes.

Two tears ran down the sides of my face
Why are you healthy in every place
Except two hard lungs inside?

Blessed oil at the door, around your bed
Companion to healing scriptures.
I am quick to say Rise up brother rise up.

Supplication Five:
I Cannot Feel Shame

I fasted food and earthly pleasures
I prayed without ceasing in known and unknown tongues
I dance liturgical warfare in the ICU bathroom
I organized a prayer chain
I telephoned every person I believed would speak to God
On your behalf
I played spirituals incessantly
I spoke hope, life, and healing through Holy Scripture
I read books on how to have a miraculous breakthrough
I touched and agreed on your outcome
I met you on a highway in my dreams and we traveled together
For a while
I praised God until my head hurt and my lips dried
I would do it all again and even more.

Supplication Six:
I Accept His Leaving

My faith spirals into the heavens to kiss your lips
To kiss the nectored lips of Jehovah
So that this one whom I love
Will yet live in paradise with you.

SUPPLICATION SEVEN:
PRAYER TO RECEIVE HIM

sh sh sh
do you still hear me God
i am small
hiding way down here
in earth's brown clay.

sh sh sh
can you hear me God
my fear
is like a beacon
to guide the angels.

sh sh sh
will you hear me God
please don't let
my beloved suffer
take your child into your Glory.

 A Single Mother's Lullaby

For my loving and forgiving son; Woodie Onkendi.

Holding you tenderly in my arms, my darling son
I beg your forgiveness as I gently caress you to sleep.
I murmur repeatedly that I love you, love you, honestly I do.
Yet I sometimes scream at the little boy that is you
when the pain really churns and convulses inside of me.
I mistakenly yell at you when the core of the problem is
the world outside my door has me frustrated and bound.

Now in the nighttime, I hold you close to my heart
and I whisper over and over in a solemn binding prayer
that I'm sorry, sorry, sorry, so sorry
to hurt the one I love in even the smallest way.
Tomorrow I'll do better when I recall that you my dearest
are young and weak and vulnerable
but all the same worthy of my protection and highest respect.

This is a single mother's lullaby to her baby, her child
carefully crooned in the sweetest spiritual love
to a truly wanted and truly loved innocent victim
to the stresses and strains, heavy, on one pair of shoulders.
From our night time talks, I promise with each day that dawns
comes a better understanding and I grow stronger,
more able to nurture and support us both.

RITUAL PREPARATION
FOR A WOMAN
INTELLECTUAL STEPPIN OUT
IN MADISON, WISCONSIN

i soak in hot scented water
thick with jasmine petals
while the sweet smells of incense float
smokily about my blue/black silhouette
and the flickers of meltin candles
situated round my bathtub's edge
throw warm light against the early night.

i step out wet onto a black sheepskin rug
bendin first to tenderly dry the beige bottoms of my feet
before movin up to caress with cloth
all the angles and circles of my flesh
my velvet-colored perfumed flesh.

i remove olive oil from a gallon jug
warm it briefly
before pourin the rich slickness in the middle of my head
and feelin it slowly sensuously slide
down my front and my back
when it reaches my ankles

i rub the oil into my hair and skin
i rub until i glimmer and shine
with burnished onyx highlights.

i look into the full length mirror
precocious head bent to one side
to puzzle over whether to wear my sable hair
nappy around my sun-kissed face
or nappy folded into thick braids
i smile flashin unblemished pearls as my curly kinks
wrap lovingly between fingers.

i praise my African body in ululation*
castin a dark voluptuous womanly reflection
well shaped head slender neck big breasts narrow waist
tight belly huge butt shapely legs and large flat feet
i begin a slow undulatin dance to soul music
while the taut skin ripples in response.
i grab a powder puff and pat talcum powder delicately
under my arms between the swells of breasts and thighs
a shower of powder falls down my back to dry
between my shoulder blades
my undergarments are black lace and vivid colored cotton
i encircle my wide hips with my favorite kanga* material.

*Ululation is an African sound expressed in celebration of
special people or events.

*Kanga is a popular type of material worn in Kenya that
includes proverbs printed in Swahili.

i lean forward into a lighted mirror
brushin gently curved eyebrows then long lashes
i trace the rim of my almond-shaped eyes with kohl
and the rim of my generous mouth with color
my full lips press the vibrant earth tones evenly.

i chew on peppermint leaves
as i feel my six senses flush with excitement
i'm goin out tonight
i've turned the computer off
i'm goin out tonight
all my books are closed
i'm goin out tonight
i fasten cowrie shells into my hair
i place precious metals in my ears
around my neck arms and ankles
i'm goin out tonight
i slip into a soft silk dress
and black patent leather high heels
to take me where i want to go
and to the man who recognizes and appreciates
the over looked beauty that is me.

OU FIT ME

A missing puzzle piece
found and fitted.

A key in a lock
that turns easily.

A right amount of current
flowing through prongs
snug in a socket.

You fit me.

UR JOURNEY

He stood concrete in his life
as I sat abstract inside mine.
We moved in cinnamon circles
that never once intersected.

He struggled in frigid Wisconsin
as I suffered In temperate Kenya.
We moved hesitantly toward
the fragrance of freedom, alone.

He vowed never to love again
as I grew content with solitude.
The day we met was scented
with possibilities.

Our journey together began in that moment,
the athlete who recites poetry
and the poet who enjoys movement.
Our journey is a sensual love affair.

 Bouquet of Magnolias

Carrying a bouquet of splendid magnolias
Curled whitish blossoms nestled in verdant waxy leaves
Yellow center surprise
Heavy fragrance permeating my life and the wedding
With southern contradictions.

I will be neither Mississippi belle nor vixen
Just my Black woman self
Wrapped in golden lace and ribbon
Cowrie shells sewn into dark braids
And a bouquet of heavenly magnolias scenting the air.

Kneeling at the altar of the Lord
Next to you, still your own Black man
Blessed by preacher, family and friends
My beloved is a bouquet of magnolias
Fragrant to me.